DATE DUE

2002

DISCARDED

PRINTED IN U.S.A.

THE HORSE LIBRARY

THE HORSE
IN WAR

BILL FELBER

CHELSEA HOUSE PUBLISHERS
PHILADELPHIA

Frontis: A mounted soldier and his horse are equipped with gas masks to handle chemical warfare in France during World War I.

CHELSEA HOUSE PUBLISHERS

EDITOR IN CHIEF Sally Cheney
ASSOCIATE EDITOR IN CHIEF Kim Shinners
PRODUCTION MANAGER Pamela Loos
ART DIRECTOR Sara Davis

STAFF FOR *THE HORSE IN WAR*

EDITOR Sally Cheney
ASSOCIATE ART DIRECTOR Takeshi Takahashi
SERIES DESIGNER Keith Trego

CHESTNUT PRODUCTIONS AND CHOPTANK SYNDICATE, INC.

EDITORIAL AND PICTURE RESEARCH Mary Hull and Norman Macht
LAYOUT AND PRODUCTION Lisa Hochstein

http://www.chelseahouse.com

First Printing

1 3 5 7 9 8 6 4 2

Library of Congress Cataloguing-in-Publication Data Applied For.

Horse Library SET: 0-7910-6650-9
The Horse in War: 0-7910-6651-7

TABLE OF CONTENTS

Francis I, king of France from 1515–1547, wore an elaborate suit of armor for this royal portrait. Francis led an army composed of French nobility in several costly wars during his reign.

RAMSES TO AGINCOURT

The origins of the cavalry horse have long been lost to antiquity. But we do know that as early as 2500 B.C., the nation-states of Assyria, Mesopotamia, Babylon, and Egypt used horses and asses to pull chariots, creating the first cavalry of record.

More than 1,000 years later, during the time of Ramses II in Egypt, the first "regular" cavalry—a trained unit of horse-drawn soldiers—was organized as a specific part of the larger standing army. These early horses were too small to carry heavily armored warriors. They were used primarily to pull chariots.

Over time, the Egyptians studied various breeds to create the best cavalry stock. Arabians were crossbred with horses from Phoenicia and other frontiers to develop a horse with great speed and endurance.

The first great cavalry tactician may have been Philip of Macedonia. By Philip's time, riders on horseback had largely replaced chariots as a strike force. But these bareback riders fought in a loose and free-form manner. Philip organized his men into units and sent them hurtling toward the enemy in a formation that would strike terror into the hearts of entrenched defenders for centuries to come—this was the cavalry charge. During the 4th century B.C., Philip's

 Inventing the Saddle and Stirrup

The saddle was first formulated by nomadic Scythian tribesmen around 700 B.C. They connected stuffed cushions with cross-straps positioned alongside the horse's spine. This transferred the rider's weight to a larger area of the horse, enabling it to run faster and with greater stability and stamina. It also reduced the incidence of saddle sores.

The stirrup, another major innovation in horsemanship and mounted warfare, may have been brought to Europe by nomadic Asian tribes. There is evidence pointing to 5th century China as the place of origin, but other evidence suggests that Persians or Mongolians may have invented the stirrup, which made it easier for a rider to keep his balance while pivoting in the saddle or shooting a bow and arrow. The stirrup did not come into common use throughout much of Europe until late in the first millennium A.D.

son, Alexander the Great, who rode a horse named Bucephalus, had employed the cavalry charge to extend Greek military dominance across most of the known world.

In the Roman military culture, which rose as Greece's dominance faded in the last three centuries B.C., horses were used largely to haul supplies for the Roman legions. When the Roman generals employed riders, they were often mercenaries hired from North African tribes. Hannibal, a Carthaginian general, taught the Romans the power of the cavalry horse. As an African from an area rich with fine Arabian stock, Hannibal knew what trained cavalry units, sitting atop animals with rippling chests, excellent speed, and wind could do. Although better known for his use of elephants, Hannibal scored a substantial victory over Roman troops around 200 B.C., largely through his effective use of cavalry.

This defeat moved the Romans to develop a larger, sturdier breed. The Roman horse had to be stronger, because, over the years, Roman cavalrymen had added more armor plating for protection, making them heavier to carry. Roman riders had not yet developed an effective saddle, so they had to direct their mounts by use of knee pressure. This limited them to handling very light weapons. It could be said that Rome's failure to adequately develop and use its cavalry contributed to its downfall. At the Battle of Adrianople in 378 B.C., when Rome confronted the invading Goths and Huns from the north, those nomadic tribes' use of saddles, lifetime of riding experience, speed, and use of mounted weaponry led to the Romans' defeat.

In October 1066, William of Normandy prepared a great force to cross the English Channel and invade England. The English, under Saxon King Harold, had never seen such a force as the one that disembarked from William's ships at

A Greek horseman of the 5th century B.C. is shown riding with spears in his fist.

Hastings. William's Norman-bred horses were huge; they had to be to support the weight they carried. The soldiers atop them wore shirts of welded iron rings known as mail. Metal helmets protected their heads. They carried long lances and heavy swords. And when they attacked, they did not dismount, as the Saxons expected. Instead, they charged on their horses.

Against this might, Harold's forces were not defenseless. They, too, wore armor, and they swung heavy battle-axes capable of slicing into the helmets and chain mail, as well as the horses. At first Harold's defenders held their own.

Soon, though, the repeated cavalry charges wore those defenses down. William's invaders forced the Saxons into retreat. Harold himself lay dead on the field of battle.

William the Conqueror's cavalry horses served as the basis for a new breed of horse, the Anglo-Normans, which would be seen on battlefields for centuries to come.

But in the age of the knight, kings and princes often differed over the best approach to building a cavalry. Our image today is of a heavily armored warrior riding into battle much as William's landing force did, atop huge mounts and carrying heavy weaponry. Others favored speed and maneuverability.

The battle of Bannockburn in 1314, between Edward II of England and the Scottish leader Robert the Bruce, was one such confrontation of styles. Unlike the English soldiers atop heavy mounts, Robert's troops rode smaller, more agile ponies. They carried a bare minimum of provisions and survived by drinking river water and eating what animals

 Bucephalus

Legend has it that Bucephalus, the horse ridden by the legendary conqueror Alexander the Great, died at the advanced age of 30 during a battle in India. Already mortally wounded, Bucephalus carried his master out of harm's way before succumbing. So grateful was Alexander that he named a city near the battle site Bucephalia in honor of his faithful horse.

they could trap. These cavalry bands could hit and run, inflicting damage while escaping it themselves, and they covered distances unthinkable to more heavily equipped armies. Although outnumbered three to one by the English, Robert's troops triumphed that day at Bannockburn in a victory for Scotland.

The best-known cavalry confrontations of this era were the series of engagements between Christian and Muslims— the Crusades, fought over 200 years in the 11th through the 13th centuries. The combined forces of Christian Europe, directed by the Pope and frequently led by kings and princes, rode off to the Middle East with the goal of evicting the Muslims from the Holy Land and returning it to Christian control.

In one important battle, the Egyptian Saladin recaptured Jerusalem using different cavalry tactics. The Crusaders, holding their lance in their right hand and a shield in their left, relied on power. They were excellent against a fixed

 Tamerlane

Tamerlane (1336–1405), a Tartar warrior who could trace his lineage to Genghis Khan, believed that the secret of a great cavalry lay in strong breeding stock. He selected the finest Arabian horses from his areas of conquest to use for breeding. As a result, Tamerlane's armies moved with a swiftness others could not hope to match. On one occasion, the king of the Turkish Empire set off with 200,000 men in search of Tamerlane. Instead of confronting the enemy, Tamerlane circled his forces behind the king, seizing the Turkish city of Ankara, and laying siege to the king's entire supply system.

enemy. But Saladin's forces did not remain fixed in one place. His lighter bands were expert riders, quicker and more effective than the Crusaders, faster to reform, and never susceptible to a charge. In addition to a lance, they carried arrows, giving them a greater striking range, as well as clubs and swords. They were prepared to fight in any circumstance, and over time they drove the occupying European forces from one city after another. Although the conflict ebbed and flowed for another two centuries, in the end the superior technique of Saladin and his successors won the day, reclaiming those territories for the Muslims.

The last great battle pitting knightly forces against one another occurred in 1415, when the victory at Agincourt by English King Henry V marked the end of the mounted, armored knight as an effective combatant.

Henry's 5,000 troops confronted a much larger French force of about 20,000. The French wore heavy armor, carried large lances and swords, and rode Boulonnais, huge horses from the Boulogne region that were bred for the Crusades. The English, aboard lighter, swifter horses, relied on arrows, enabling them to fight from a greater distance. Even in close combat, their lighter armor, combined with lighter weaponry (mostly daggers and swords) gave them greater flexibility. British arrows created havoc among the French, killing many of the horses and wounding others, rendering them difficult to control. When the French dismounted they were often trampled by their own horses or by those in the ranks behind them. For three hours the fighting continued, and in the end Henry's forces routed the French. Injured horses well enough to recover without much care were laden with booty and sent back behind the lines. The more seriously injured were shot so they would not become a burden to the army itself.

2

To stand up to the new firearms of the 1600s, armor had to be made even tougher and heavier than before. To compensate for the extra weight all but the most essential pieces of armor were discarded.

FROM CAVALIERS TO CAVALRY

B etween Agincourt and the 17th century, cavalry forces frequently played a supporting role to the infantry. But during Britain's "Glorious Revolution" of the 1640s, the cavalry again rose to a prominent battlefield role as Charles I's Cavaliers clashed with the Roundheads—so named for the look of their helmets—of the revolutionary leader, Oliver Cromwell.

The favorite tactic of the king's Cavaliers was a close charge, with sabers raised. Cromwell adopted the "feint and assault" tactic developed by the Swedish king Gustavus Adolphus. Such an assault relied on creating movement in one direction, only to respond in another, throwing the defenders off balance.

Cromwell defeated the King and became lord protector of England. One of his first acts was to improve the breeding stock of the country's horses.

Around this same time, there was a rise of riding schools across Europe. Military leaders gradually honed the skills of their cavalrymen into specialties. The "dragoons" and "lancers" rode swifter horses for mobility, while the "cuirassiers"—named after the breastplates they wore— took the heavier mounts. Two great commanders applied these varied forces with unusual skill and daring. The first was Frederick the Great, the Prussian leader of the mid-18th century. Frederick's dragoons became known for their combat skill against the Russians and Austrians in numerous battles between 1755 and 1760. At Zorndorf in 1758, Frederick threw his cavalry against deeply entrenched Russian infantry and routed them from their positions, achieving an unexpected victory. This victory and others like it allowed Frederick's Prussian forces to control almost all of Europe east of France.

 Richard III

In William Shakespeare's play Richard III, King Richard's army is being routed by the army of the soon-to-be King Henry VII at the 1485 Battle of Bosworth Field. His horse has just been killed beneath him. Having fallen to the ground with his horse dead under him, Richard gazes at the battle around him, and cries helplessly, "A horse, a horse, my kingdom for a horse." But there is no horse for Richard to mount and to continue his fight. A short time later, still horseless, Richard is cornered by another combatant and slain.

**A French engraving from 1733 depicts the "airs above the ground,"
advanced dressage maneuvers that were taught at cavalry schools.
Today these moves are performed by Lipizzaner horses only.**

The second memorable leader of the time, Napoleon, favored Arabian horses for the breeding of cavalry mounts. He established riding schools that taught cavalry skills along with character and disposition, both of horse and rider. Horses were schooled in gymnastics for improved movement in combat, and in dressage, which is presentation under battle conditions. As a result, Napoleon's cavalry excelled in balance, rhythm, and movement.

His grand army relied on three separate waves of cavalry. The advance guard was the four divisions of dragoons, the lighter cavalry that struck at the enemy with close-range fire. His cuirassiers—which generally numbered 14 separate regiments—swept through the often-dazed ground forces. Two regiments of carabiniers, heavy units generally identical to the cuirassiers, supplemented the cuirassiers. Napoleon often called on his division of lancers for a final, decisive sweep of the enemy's remaining troops. All of

Napoleon I, emperor of the French from 1769-1821, used cavalry to conquer Italy and Egypt in the late 18th century.

these troops were trained to close on the enemy at a programmed pace, first at a trot, then a canter, and finally—over the final 150 yards—at a gallop.

These tactics made Napoleon the world's most dominant military figure. Twice, however, superior horsemanship defeated him. The first was in his confrontation with

Cossack riders during his 1812 invasion of Russia. The second occurred when the English general Wellington out-maneuvered him in 1815 at Waterloo, destroying the French force.

Mounted fighting units played little part in the American Revolution. Regular cavalry operated only sporadically, not only during the Revolution but also for many years there-after, and usually for specific missions. When the mission was completed, the cavalry was often disbanded, and its soldiers returned to their farms and fields. Nonetheless, at critical times both during the Revolution and later during the War of 1812, cavalry forces rose to the defense of the new American nation. The 5th Connecticut Regiment of Light Horse Militia was crucial to Washington's successful retreat following his army's defeat in the battle for New York. The Philadelphia City Troop of Light Horse rode with Washington during his famed surprise Christmas attack on the Hessians at Trenton. Washington was so impressed by the contributions of this unit to the Trenton victory that he immediately asked the Continental

 General Pulaski

The first commander of an American cavalry corps wasn't even an American. He was a Polish nobleman, Count Casimir Pulaski, who had come to the rebelling colonies after the Russians con-fiscated his lands back home. He fought with such distinction in the Battle of Brandywine that he was commissioned a brigadier general and permitted to organize a cavalry force. On October 9, 1779, Pulaski was mortally wounded in a battle with the British near Charleston, South Carolina.

Congress for permission to raise a cavalry force of 3,000 comprising four regiments. These units—the 1st through 4th Continental Light Dragoons—represented the first true American cavalry.

The new cavalry units found arms, horses, and uniforms wherever they could locate them. Some wore the colors of various state militia with which they had previously served; one unit was even outfitted with uniforms taken from the British, an unfortunate decision that led to dangerous confusion when those troops took to the battlefield. Most of the units carried broadswords or sabers, but only a lucky few were armed with handguns, which were hard to get. Muskets—primitive rifles—often served instead.

The Continental Cavalry fought in most of the Revolutionary theaters, including the defenses of New York

 ## The Flamboyant Hussars

The word Hussar comes from a Hungarian word meaning "twenty;" it refers to a time when Hungarian lords were required to equip one cavalryman for every 20 acres of land they controlled. The Hussars dressed in bright reds and blues and wore fur hats. They rode swift, light horses—often the shagya, a horse that was half Arab and half Hungarian—and brandished sabers and pistols. Their dashing appearance and flamboyant reputation quickly became a model for "Hussar" units in other nations' armies.

and Philadelphia, at Saratoga, the Hudson River campaign, and in the battles of King's Mountain and Cowpens. Although they were not a primary force during the decisive action at Yorktown, about 100 members of the 4th Continental Dragoon accompanied Washington's march to confront Cornwallis.

For the next 30 years, Congress authorized temporary cavalry units for specific campaigns: to protect settlers against Indian attacks, and to fight the British in the War of 1812. As each crisis ended, the cavalry was disbanded.

Mounted on his horse, Winfield Scott, General in Chief of the U.S.
Army, reviews the troops in 1846. At the start of the Mexican War,
the U.S. Army had two cavalry regiments, and soon added a third.
The Mexican War is considered the nation's first largely cavalry-
fought war.

MEXICO AND
THE PUSH WEST

A merica looked westward in the 1830s. The nation's dyn-amic president, Andrew Jackson, a backwoodsman from Tennessee, envisioned the nation spreading across the Great Plains and beyond. But Jackson, also a soldier-hero of the War of 1812, knew that hopes of such settlement would be futile without the military means to protect the migrating settlers.

Jackson's secretary of war, Lewis Cass, campaigned for the creation of a regular cavalry. "Mounted troops are absolutely necessary for the defense of that part of the inland frontier in contact with the Indian tribes," Cass wrote in a message to Congress. In response, Congress passed a bill creating six companies of about 100 men each, authorizing one dollar a day in pay, with the men providing their own horses. Thus was born the first Regiment of Dragoons; the second Regiment of Dragoons followed in 1836. It wasn't much, but it was the first American cavalry in 17 years.

Those first cavalry units and their immediate successors were assigned to the Western frontier outposts to protect the settlers. Their provisions were poor, their quarters sometimes non-existent, and their uniforms rag-tag. Some were given weapons that had not been removed from storage since the War of 1812. When Congress created that first regiment of dragoons in 1833, it failed to fund horses for three of the five companies. In the frontier forts, typhus, dysentery, and other debilitating diseases were constant threats. With all those problems, morale quickly sank.

Throughout the 1830s, cavalry units were assigned the duty of escorting Indian tribes westward from their lands in advance of the arriving settlers. Not infrequently, combat resulted, as in the second Seminole War fought in Florida between 1835 and 1842. The trouble began when the Seminoles repudiated an agreement signed by their elders, by which they were to be relocated west of the Mississippi River, and massacred a force of U.S. infantry. In the first year of the conflict, more than 150 companies of mounted troops were created in the effort to quell the threat. The most decisive moment of the drawn-out conflict occurred on Christmas day in 1837 when a mixed force of cavalry and infantry under the command of Colonel Zachary Taylor dealt a severe blow to the Seminoles. The Indians and cavalry engaged in sporadic guerrilla battles for five years.

By the start of the Mexican War in 1846, the U.S. Army included two regiments of cavalry; Congress soon agreed to President Polk's request for a third regiment. Mexico put

New York lithographer Nathan Currier depicted the Battle of Buena Vista, fought on February 23, 1847, in this hand-colored mass-produced print, which he sold to Americans anxious for scenes of the far-flung war with Mexico.

14 active mounted units in the field, supplemented by six mounted militia units. Although the U.S. mounted force numbered only three regiments, two were battle-hardened by their experience with the Indians.

These units were often augmented by mounted state militia forces. One such unit, the Missouri Mounted Volunteers, was commanded by Colonel Alexander Doniphan, a frontier lawyer whose lack of military experience did not prevent him from conducting one of the most remarkable extended cavalry campaigns ever recorded. It was a journey made even more remarkable by the fact that this unit of state militia lacked almost all of the requisites of military life: they had no tents, no uniforms, no quartermaster, no supply train, and little training in military discipline. But they were tough men of the land, natural riders, and even more natural fighters.

First Doniphan and his 900 men rode from Missouri to an area west of Santa Fe in what was then Mexican territory, where they subdued a revolt by the Navajo nation. Once that was done, they turned southward toward Chihuahua, only to be attacked on Christmas Day by a force of 1,300 Mexicans near what is now El Paso. They picked the attackers apart with their superior marksmanship, then conducted a series of mounted sorties into the enemy's ranks that forced a Mexican retreat barely more than a half hour after the first shots were fired.

Now supplemented by some artillery pieces and a few volunteers they had met along the way, Doniphan's force arrived in Chihuahua late in February 1847 and were met by nearly 4,000 soldiers, cavalry, infantry, artillerymen, and machete-wielding troops. Staying out of the artillery's range, Doniphan outflanked the Mexican line, then attacked it from the rear, picking it apart with mounted charges as well as confrontations on foot. The Mexicans suffered substantial losses and surrendered their city two days later. Doniphan's own casualties amounted to one dead and seven wounded. Not content with that accomplishment, Doniphan immediately marshaled his troops to join General Taylor's main force more than 500 miles away.

Units from the First and Second Dragoons played roles in the two decisive battles of the Mexican War, Buena Vista and Vera Cruz. The battle of Buena Vista pitted Taylor against Mexican General Santa Anna—the man who had taken the Alamo a decade earlier. Taylor's force included one squadron each from the First and Second, along with various state militia units, most of which were assigned the task of holding the army's flanks. They were not up to it, and were quickly pushed back by the Mexicans, who threatened to collapse the American line in on itself. The First Cavalry Dragoons buttressed the line and held it firm. As a result, Buena Vista, which might have been an American defeat, concluded as a draw. The two sides combined suffered nearly 3,200 dead, wounded, or missing.

Elements of the First and Second Dragoons, along with a newly raised regiment of Mounted Riflemen, disembarked with General Winfield Scott at the port of Vera Cruz about a week later, and launched a drive toward Mexico City that concluded with Scott leading his troops into the city's square in September.

The Mounted Riflemen, who were forced to walk during much of this campaign (having lost many of their horses during the sea voyage), earned a special place in military lore during Scott's capture of Mexico City. They attacked and captured Chapultepec Castle the day before the arrival of Scott's main force. When the General marched his units into the Mexican capital 24 hours later, he was greeted by the Riflemen, their own flag flying from the flagpole at the National Palace. So moved was the general that he bowed low to the soldiers, saluting them and saying, "Brave Rifles! Veterans! You have been baptized in fire and blood and have come out steel."

The soldiers rode home in triumph and found new demands awaiting them. Gold had been discovered in California, setting in motion a great migration westward

The Charge of the Light Brigade

The most famous cavalry engagement of the 19th century occurred half a world away from the United States in the Crimean peninsula of present-day Russia. Thanks to a poem written by Alfred Lord Tennyson, a charge made by the Light Brigade in 1854 during the battle for Balaclava in the Crimean War became the single most-remembered cavalry action in all of recorded history. The famous phrase "Theirs not to reason why, theirs but to do and die," comes from Tennyson's The Charge of the Light Brigade.

The Light Brigade, a unit of fewer than 700 mounted British cavalry under the command of Lord Cardigan, was part of a British force positioned at one end of a long valley framed on the other three sides by Russian cannons. The order came down for the Light Brigade to attack a Russian infantry formation, but it was misunderstood and the brigade instead set off at a charge through the valley against the artillery unit at the far end. The result was a slaughter. The astonished Russian gunners nearly obliterated the valiant horses and riders as they charged through what Tennyson called "the Valley of Death." When the attack concluded, fewer than 200 members of the brigade were able to return to the British lines.

One who made it back was Lord Cardigan himself, riding atop his steed, Ronald. When Ronald died, Lord Cardigan had the horse's head preserved and mounted in a glass case at his home. Today the Charge of the Light Brigade is remembered as both an exhibition of the undeniable bravery of cavalry troops against impossible odds, and as an illustration of the folly of mass cavalry charges against fixed artillery units. A French general who witnessed the charge summed up what had transpired this way: "C'est magnifique, mais ce n'est pas guerre." ("It was magnificent, but it was not war.")

that demanded mounted forces for protection all the way to the Pacific. To the south, the Santa Fe Trail needed guarding against Indians and outlaw raiders. The march to Oregon and the Northwest posed a third demand. New forts took shape to protect travelers along these trails. In 1848, there were only nine such forts along the frontier; by 1860, that number had increased to more than five dozen, located in every state and territory west of the Mississippi.

Killed by a rebel shell, a horse lies dead in the field after the Battle of Gettysburg in July 1863. The horse is still hitched to the Federal gun carriage it drew to the battlefield.

4

THE CAVALRY IN THE CIVIL WAR

Against new artillery and repeating rifles, the charging cavalryman's gleaming saber was no match. With the invention of the Gatling gun in 1861, stationary troops could bring down a quickly advancing cavalry in a hail of bullets fired at rates of between 350 and 1,200 per minute.

Due to this new battlefield reality, officers converted their cavalry units from front-line forces to raiders, so the cavalry advantages of speed and maneuverability could still be put to effective use. This was the role of the cavalry in the Civil War.

The South, an agrarian and riding society, had access to more and better horses. Many Northerners came from large cities.

A Union artillery unit poses with its cannons and horses in this photograph, taken between 1861 and 1864 by the field staff of Civil War photographer Matthew Brady.

This proved a liability for the Union cavalry. Union officers estimated that it took two years to train a cavalryman from scratch, considering that a good cavalryman had to be an efficient warrior either mounted or dismounted, and had to understand the needs of his horse. If a trooper gave his horse too little food or water, the horse would break down, as many did. It was estimated that the Union army went through about 284,000 horses in the war's first years to outfit 60,000 men in the field—an average of nearly five horses per man—on the other hand, riders also had to guard against overfeeding or overwatering. Supplies were too scarce to be wasted. In all these matters, the more experienced Confederate riders began with an advantage.

The first great battle of the war, Bull Run, illustrated the Southern superiority on horseback. General Irwin McDowell's Northern force of 36,000 men was slightly larger than the 32,000 Southerners confronting it, but could muster only seven companies of cavalry. Against them, the South presented the 1st Virginia Cavalry Regiment, a superb troupe under the leadership of Jeb Stuart, a mounted battalion led by Colonel Wade Hampton, and additional companies. As the battle turned toward the Southern side, Union forces began a retreat, pursued aggressively by Stuart's chargers. McDowell lacked the mounted manpower to counter. In short order, the retreat turned into a route. Stuart's men chased the Union soldiers almost all the way back to Washington.

If Bull Run had any value to the Northern cause, it was to spur recruitment; within a month of the battle, more than 30 new Union cavalry regiments were in uniform and

 ## A Divided Cavalry

Nearly 300 of the Union army's force of about 1,100 professional officers resigned their commissions at the start of the Civil War to join the Southern cause. The toll was particularly high among cavalry units, which lost more than half of their officers to the South, including Jeb Stuart, Thomas Jackson, and Joe Johnston. At the time of the war's start, the North was left with only one cavalry officer with the rank of colonel.

Confederate General Robert E. Lee poses on his horse, Traveler.

training to join the fight. By year's end, the number of new cavalry regiments had swollen to more than 80.

The war was hard on riders and horses. Although manning tables called for regiments to consist of between 1,300 and 1,400 personnel, in practice, the effective fighting force was often barely half that in number. Because they were easy targets, horses suffered the most. Regiments might be assigned one veterinary surgeon, and each company was fortunate if it had two farriers, or blacksmiths, within its ranks.

Cavalry battles were rare. On June 9, 1863, perhaps the largest cavalry battle ever waged on the American continent broke out in northern Virginia. A federal cavalry force commanded by Alfred Pleasanton confronted Jeb Stuart's main force of 12,000 men for more than two hours at a place called Brandy Station. The event was preceded by pomp reminiscent of great cavalry battles of long ago. Four days before the combat, Stuart's army marched in a grand public review attended by Confederate dignitaries, governors of several states, and the region's most beautiful women, attired in the best gowns. When the battle did occur on the very same parade ground, both sides sustained heavy casualties. Pleasanton finally withdrew his men, believing (incorrectly) that he had crippled Stuart's force.

An 1864 photograph of U.S. General Ulysses S. Grant shows him standing alongside his war horse, Cincinnati.

The North was to find out differently in less than a month's time when Stuart's men proved one of the toughest of the Southern units at the battle of Gettysburg.

But these battles were coincidental; they occurred because units happened upon one another, not because they sought each other out in organized conflict. Cavalry troops were far more likely to be assigned one of several less glamorous tasks: scouting, raiding, or foraging.

In these skills, Jeb Stuart was one of the best. In 1862, under orders from General Robert E. Lee to scout the position and strength of Northern General George McClellan's Army of the Potomac, Stuart and 1,000 of his men completed an entire circle of the main Northern force, capturing 165 men and 260 horses and mules, and providing Lee with valuable intelligence—all with the loss of only one man. Later that year, Stuart again rode behind enemy lines to inflict great damage. Again, the Army of the Potomac was the target. The information Stuart brought back aided Lee in his preparations for the Second Battle of Bull Run, in which the Southerners routed the Union army.

Perhaps the most famous of the raiders was Colonel John S. Mosby, a Virginia attorney, who volunteered at the war's outset and eventually won command of the 43rd Battalion of Virginia Cavalry. History more familiarly recalls these troopers as Mosby's Rangers. Seldom operating in groups of more than a dozen, soldiers of Mosby's battalion brought down communication lines, disrupted and ransacked supply trains, harassed Union troops, and once kidnapped Brigadier General Edwin H. Stoughton from his own headquarters in Fairfax, Virginia. They rode and struck across a wide range, but were most comfortable in northern Virginia, an area along the Shenandoah River that became known as Mosby's Confederacy. There, Mosby could count on the sheltering protection of the sympathetic residents while carrying out his raids on the Union army.

Not all soldiers conducted themselves with traditional military decorum, and this proved a particular problem in the cavalry. As the cavalry mission developed into one that at times more closely resembled piracy, some mounted units attracted men that could best be described as bandits. Charles Quantrill led one such band. Quantrill was a Missouri gambler-turned-raider who received a captain's commission in the Confederate army despite a background that included murder and horse stealing. On an August day in 1863, Quantrill led his band into the city of Lawrence, Kansas, slaughtering 150 men, women, and children, many on the town's main street. One of Quantrill's raiders that bloody day was a young ne'er-do-well, skilled both atop a mount and with a gun, named Jesse James. James would later become one of America's most notorious outlaws.

Although the Union cavalry began the war with several disadvantages, they were helped when Kentucky, a slave-holding state, elected not to secede. Kentucky was perhaps

 The McClellan Saddle

Until the 1830s, the U.S. Army did not even provide saddles for its mounted troops; they were expected to bring their own. In 1859 an American army officer named George McClellan designed a new type of saddle modeled after those he had seen in Europe. The McClellan saddle went through many updates and modernizations, but it continued in use until the horse cavalry itself ceased to exist in the 1940s.

the single best breeding ground for horses in the nation, and by the war's middle years it supplied thousands of the finest quality mounts to the Union cause.

The North also had at least one leader who was the equal of those leading the Confederate cavalry. In March 1864, General U.S. Grant called on one of his trusted lieutenants, Major General Phil Sheridan, to reorganize and command the cavalry of the Army of the Potomac. At the time, the cavalry consisted of 20,000 men, 12,000 of them in the saddle, and was used mostly for patrol or scout duties. Sheridan complained to General George Meade of what he considered this misuse of a resource, adding that he could catch and defeat Stuart if given the chance. Meade repeated this boast to Grant, who is said to have matter-of-factly replied, "Then let him go out and do it."

Sheridan had no cavalry training. He was a West Point graduate and a career infantry officer. But with Grant's support, he quickly changed the Union cavalry from a

 # The Yellowlegs

It may not sound like a very complimentary term for a warrior, but American cavalrymen of the 19th century took pride in being known as "Yellowlegs." The term stemmed from an Army decision to assign each branch a "color" that would make soldiers' assignments readily identifiable in the field. Soldiers of the infantry, artillery, and cavalry each wore different colored stockings and head ornaments. Yellow was the color assigned to the cavalry. Although the use of colors to identify military branches did not last, the term did; for as long as there was a mounted cavalry, cavalrymen were known as yellowlegs.

little-used appendage to a central part of the war effort. During the 1864 Battle of the Wilderness, Sheridan pulled 10,000 of his troops from the main battle area, circled Lee's army, and staged a drive toward Richmond. He knew this would force Stuart to break his cavalry away from Lee's defending force, creating the opportunity for a head-to-head battle, and that was exactly what happened.

On May 11 at a place called Yellow Tavern, Sheridan got his showdown with Stuart's 4,500 men. General George A. Custer, commanding one of Sheridan's brigades, detected a weakness in the Confederate line and attacked. In the battle that ensued, Stuart was mortally wounded and his force dispersed.

For the next several months, Sheridan fought a series of costly engagements against what was left of the Confederate force; each encounter was brief but bloody. The Union cavalry suffered more than 5,000 casualties, but Southern casualties were high as well, both in men and horses. Day by day, the South grew weaker.

On April 1, 1865, Sheridan sent the full weight of his command against Lee's battered right flank near Petersburg, Virginia. Nearly surrounded and facing starvation, Lee reluctantly marched his force westward in search of sup-plies. The Northern cavalry picked at him virtually without response. On April 8, Custer's Third Cavalry drew in front of Lee at Appomattox, halting his march. A few days later Lee surrendered to Grant.

Wearing a loincloth and moccasins, a Nez Perce warrior poses on horseback for American photographer Edward S. Curtis in 1910. By this time, all Indian tribes in the United States had been relocated to reservations.

5

FRONTIER
CAMPAIGNS

Following the Civil War, the development of the railroad pushed the frontier westward into the Dakotas, Colorado, Montana, New Mexico, and Arizona territories.

To meet the security needs this expansion created, President Andrew Johnson signed an order doubling the number of cavalry regiments from four to eight. Union Generals William Sherman and Phil Sheridan sent the bulk of the cavalry westward to protect the settlements and the railroad from Indian attack. "I am of the belief that the Indians require to be soundly whipped," Sherman instructed Sheridan. The latter entrusted much of the task to one of his own key Civil War lieutenants,

George Custer, who was placed in command of the newly formed 7th Cavalry.

This newly expanded force took up positions at dozens of forts sprinkled across the Great Plains close to the tribes judged most likely to be troublesome: Cheyenne, Crow, Blackfoot, and especially the Sioux, whose reservation occupied most of the western half of present-day South Dakota. Soldiers would ride out from these of forts on patrols that lasted days, weeks, and even months at a time. Between 1857 and 1890, the cavalry fought major engagements with Indian troops 32 times in 14 Western states.

It would not be uncommon for cavalry troops to cover 1,500 miles during a year's patrols. The life was spartan, even if no Indians were encountered. Diaries tell of long rides over barren country, through snow, ice and cold, carrying what rations they could and living off the land for the rest of their needs, with no opportunity for rest or recuperation.

 Garrison Life

The routine of the typical calvaryman consisted of reveille, drill, guard mounts, fatigue duty, and taps. Fatigue duty might involve weeding the parade ground, police details, or chopping wood for fireplaces. Cavalrymen were also responsible for maintaining their own horses and equipment. Since the frontier posts were isolated, troops had to provide their own entertainment. This often consisted of drinking or gambling. Some formed theater groups and staged plays. Temperance societies, whose members pledged not to drink, were familiar organizations. Because steady supplies of food were scarce, soldiers often tended gardens or kept small herds of livestock.

The 9th U.S. Cavalry was one of two segregated all-black cavalry regiments of "Buffalo Soldiers," as the Native Americans called them.

Life in the forts was often dull. In the rapidly expanding force, many of the new recruits were poorly trained riders, and they received little or no additional training. This was due in part to the necessity of employing the soldiers in the task of constructing the expanding network of forts. "An officer cannot have proper discipline in his command under such circumstances," observed one recruit to the 7th Cavalry stationed at Fort Harker, Kansas. Men who did not follow the rules had to clean out the stables as punishment. The pay for a cavalry soldier, $16 per month in 1865, reduced to $13 per month in 1872, and often late in coming, was not a great incentive. The food was poor.

Buffalo Soldiers of the 25th Infantry, some of them wearing buffalo robes, pose at Fort Keogh, Montana. A memorial to the deeds of the Buffalo Soldiers stands in Fort Riley, Kansas, home of the U.S. Cavalry.

Desertion was a common problem. Combining that factor with deaths and discharges, it has been estimated that the cavalry turnover rate was between 25 and 40 percent per year in the late 1860s and 1870s.

When the soldiers on patrol crossed paths with Indians, the meeting was rarely friendly. This diary entry from a soldier of the 7th Cavalry, dated November 26, 1868, describes one such encounter, the Battle of the Washita, in cold and clinical detail:

> Marched to north fork of Washita River, where we found Indian encampment; rested until daybreak and then broke in upon Black Kettle's band of Cheyenne Indians, killing a large number of warriors together with their stock; captured their women and

children and a large amount of arms and ammunition and utterly destroyed their village and winter supplies. 30 miles.

This is but a small incident of a small portion of one cavalry campaign against the Plains Indians. Few were pitched battles, because the Indian warriors, usually outnumbered in an open fight but far more familiar with the terrain, tried to engage the soldiers only on their own terms. This meant using the element of surprise, attacking in smaller but more mobile bands and riding smaller, swifter ponies to strike, inflict damage, and then out-run the cavalry whose own mounts were built for endurance rather than speed. In contrast, a cavalry soldier outfitted for routine patrol meant at least a 250-pound load for his mount.

Another consideration limited the cavalry's speed and mobility. The larger cavalry horses could not live off native grass and required dietary supplements of grains such as oats. This meant that longer patrols were often linked to supply trains; a raiding Indian party, by contrast, could travel lightly.

In the 1870s, as the ranks of cavalry swelled to meet the demands of Western expansion, many African-American men signed up. Two regiments—the 9th and 10th—were formed for black cavalry soldiers only. They were often given the filthiest jobs and forced to use the worst equipment, yet the men of these regiments quickly distinguished themselves on the field of battle. In short order they became known by the name the Indians gave them—Buffalo Soldiers—a reference to their short, wiry hair and their fierce fighting spirit.

In some respects the cavalry offered an appealing life to a black man who could ride a horse in 1870s America. Among other things, a position in the U.S. Calvary gave the

A Currier and Ives lithograph from 1876 depicts Major General George Custer at the Battle of Little Big Horn, where the entire U.S. force—save one cavalry horse—was killed.

black cavalry soldier the chance to learn to read—something that the black population of America was often not afforded at that time. Being a calvary soldier was an honorable activity in which one could earn a paycheck and the chance for promotion. As a result, desertion rates were remarkably low, and re-enlistment rates were unusually high.

The Buffalo Soldiers proved their mettle in several battles, perhaps none more memorable than during the Victorio War of 1879. Victorio was a chief of a large band of renegade Apaches in New Mexico. Ninth Cavalry Buffalo Soldiers first chased Victorio and his men across the border into Mexico. Anticipating Victorio would try to reenter the country, they relocated forces at all the various watering holes along the west Texas border and waited. The tactic worked: Victorio's forces were confronted and driven back into Mexico, never to be a force in the United States again. Between their creation in 1866 and the end of the Spanish-American War in 1898, 16 Buffalo Soldiers were awarded the Congressional Medal of Honor for heroism.

In 1869, Custer and 57 of his men from the 7th Cavalry rode into an Arapaho camp and persuaded the tribal leaders to sign a peace treaty. In March of that same year, the general rode with 800 men against a village of Cheyenne. Two white women were being held captive by the village at the time. Custer entered the camp, seized three of the tribal chiefs, and threatened to hang them if he did not get what he wanted. The Cheyenne village promptly released the two women and signed an agreement to move from their village onto a government-designated reservation.

 Comanche

From the entire force that fought with Custer at the Battle of Little Big Horn, only one creature survived—Comanche, a horse ridden into the fight by Captain Miles Keogh. On his return to Fort Riley, the commander of the 7th Cavalry issued an order: Comanche was to be given "a special and comfortable stable, and he will not be ridden by any person whomsoever, under any circumstances, nor will he be put to any kind of work." When Comanche died in 1891 at age 30, Professor L.L. Dyche of the University of Kansas took possession of the horse's body, which he had stuffed and mounted. It remains on display at the Dyche Museum of History at the University of Kansas.

Comanche, the only survivor of the Custer Massacre at Little Big Horn in 1876, stands with a uniformed cavalryman in 1887. Comanche belonged to the 7th U.S. Cavalry and was cared for at Fort Riley until his death in 1891.

In 1875, following the discovery of gold on the Sioux reservation in the Black Hills of South Dakota, the government ordered the Sioux to leave their land, and sent the 7th Cavalry to nearby Fort Abraham Lincoln to enforce the order. This precipitated the campaign that included the Battle of the Little Big Horn, in which Custer and his entire force of 211 soldiers, Indian scouts, and civilians were killed.

Within a bit more than a decade, all of the Indian tribes had been placed on reservations. One of the final eruptions occurred at Wounded Knee, South Dakota, late in 1890 when a force of about 120 Sioux appeared on the verge of rebellion against their restrictions. Troopers from a half dozen cavalry units moved into the agitated camp to disarm the Indian warriors. They were met by gunfire. The cavalry returned the fire, and an artillery unit provided support. The toll was more than 200 Indians killed or wounded, along with 75 soldiers. It took two weeks before officers and tribal leaders were able to negotiate a surrender. With the conclusion of the Wounded Knee fighting, the cavalry's role in the Indian wars essentially came to an end.

U.S. Army Signal Corps radio communications specialists of the 1940s work in the field while a packhorse stands by with their equipment.

RIDING INTO THE SUNSET

Like every summer day in Cuba, July 1, 1898 dawned oppressively hot. But Lieutenant Colonel Theodore Roosevelt and his Rough Riders didn't mind the heat. From the day of their formation in San Antonio, Texas, less than two months earlier, the nearly 1,000-strong 1st Volunteer Cavalry regiment had trained for this time and this place.

Now, as the sun broke, they prepared to put that training to use, first on Kettle Hill, then on the more imposing San Juan Hill a short distance away. In about three hours, the Rough Riders would share all of the experiences of cavalry across the ages. They would charge a heavily armed and entrenched enemy, sustain fearful casualties from bullets and heat, and they would persevere.

Spurred by the nation-wide fever that had risen since the destruction of the United States battleship *Maine* the previous February in Havana harbor, the volunteers, under the command of Colonel Leonard Wood (Roosevelt was his executive officer), had answered the call of the newly-declared war with Spain.

Aside from patriotism, the only other thing these volunteers had in common was a keen ability to ride. They were Western cowboys and ranchers, gamblers, sportsmen from the East, Ivy Leaguers, municipal policemen, Native Americans, and soldiers of fortune. More than a few of them were of questionable reputation, and they saw the Army as a chance for legal adventure.

The Rough Riders and their horses landed in Cuba on June 22, 1898, to national celebrity. They were the first Army forces on the island, and newspaper correspondents from all the major publications came along to cover their exploits. The reporters did not have long to wait; in an initial skirmish, eight Rough Riders were killed and another 34 wounded. Some criticized the combat as unnecessary, saying the Spanish had already decided to pull back. But when Colonel Wood was promoted to brigadier general on June 23 and transferred, he told reporters he viewed those earlier scraps as vital. "Such experience as we had is a quick teacher," he said.

With Roosevelt now in command, the Rough Riders attracted national attention. Not yet 40 years old, "Teddy" was already well known as a former New York state lawmaker, author, frontiersman, and Assistant Secretary of the Navy for President McKinley. One of the chief advocates of confronting Spain, he had resigned his Naval position in

Lieutenant Colonel Theodore Roosevelt leads a band of Rough Riders up Cuba's San Juan Hill on July 1, 1898, during the Spanish-American War.

May 1898 because, he explained, "I should feel distinctly ashamed . . . if I now failed to practice what I have preached."

Roosevelt mobilized his force of about 400 men. Breakfast of coffee and bacon was followed by walks through the thick underbrush that provided some cover at the base of Kettle Hill. In the dense cover, even before the first shot had been fired, heat and exhaustion were already factors. At one o'clock, the Rough Riders received their orders: Advance in support of the regular cavalry assaulting Kettle Hill.

His troopers moved quickly, often too quickly for the regulars they were supposed to be supporting. Approaching one such unit, Roosevelt told its officers, "If you don't want to go forward, let my men pass." Some of that unit's officers and men moved out with the Rough Riders as they climbed the hill toward the often unseen enemy, bullets that whizzed past them—some striking home. Within moments, Roosevelt's forces stood triumphant atop the hill.

But they did not linger there. Roosevelt saw a line of infantry laboring up nearby San Juan Hill under heavy fire from the Spanish defenders. He led his men toward a spur of the hill that was heavily laced with Spanish trenches. Two of the defenders fired at Roosevelt; he returned fire with his Colt revolver and killed one. Moving swiftly, the Rough Riders advanced to the top of the hill where they unfurled the yellow flag of the cavalry, claiming the battle-field's high ground.

It had been a costly few hours for the Rough Riders: 86 dead or wounded, six missing, and another several dozen felled by heat prostration. Yet Roosevelt's force had succeeded in its mission of capturing both hills. It had demonstrated the overwhelming strength of cavalry from time immemorial—the ability to strike swiftly upon an entrenched force. Almost immediately, Roosevelt's Rough Riders became American heroes and their capture of San Juan Hill perhaps the most memorable moment of the Spanish-American War.

It may also have been the last moment of glory for a storied military institution, the cavalry.

In addition to fighting in Cuba, turn-of-the-century U.S. cavalry units fought in the Philippines and China. In 1899, the U.S. cavalry helped quell a Philippines insurrection against the new American government. The cavalrymen, who rode frequent day and night patrols, brought with them new weaponry, a .30 caliber Krag repeating carbine that replaced the old .45 caliber Springfield rifles which had become famous during the Indian wars.

At about the same time, eight troops from the 6th Cavalry were sent to China to protect American interests during the Boxer Rebellion. The cavalry played an important role in settling that conflict, capturing the walled city of Tientsin. It was a key to ending the Boxers' 55-day siege of Peking and eventually the rebellion itself.

In June 1916, cavalry troops under the command of General John Pershing rode south out of Columbus, New Mexico, crossed the border with Mexico, and set out to capture the outlaw Pancho Villa. This attack, which became known as the Punitive Expedition, was in reprisal for a raid on Columbus in which Villa and his men burned the town and killed 18 Americans.

General Pershing's troops rode hundreds of miles through some of the most difficult conditions any cavalry unit had ever encountered. In the heat of summer, the desert was dry and barren, with little forage for the horses and little water for the horses or riders. Outlaws and Indians were every-where and posed a threat to the troops. Pershing's army also had to fight the Mexican army, which resented the invading Americans.

 Cavalry School

The nation's first school for teaching cavalry officers and their horses opened at Fort Riley, Kansas, in 1892. Its curriculum consisted of study and practice in two distinct areas: hippology and equitation. Hippology, the study of horses, was a textbook course designed to teach the mounted officer how to preserve and protect the animal beneath him. Riding lessons, called equitation classes, were designed to improve the officer's riding skills.

On June 21, 1916, a unit of 76 cavalrymen of the black 10th Cavalry—the Buffalo Soldiers—confronted an entrenched force of 400 Mexicans armed with machine guns. The 10th charged headlong across open ground into the Mexican fire, crashing into the Mexican lines. Casualties

The legend of Lieutenant Colonel Teddy Roosevelt's charge up San Juan Hill in 1898 helped him become Vice President of the United States two years later; when President McKinley was assassinated in September 1901, Roosevelt became the 26th President of the United States.

were heavy on both sides. Eventually the superior numbers of the Mexican defenders won out, but before surrendering, the men of the 10th Cavalry inflicted more casualties on the Mexicans than they themselves suffered. The Punitive Expedition to capture Pancho Villa is considered the last major cavalry effort by American troops.

The arrival of motorized vehicles in the early 20th century accelerated the phase out of cavalry. Yet during the two great conflicts of the first half of that century, the mounted soldier and his horse still saw occasional duty.

The horse's most vital role during World War I was as a draft and pack animal. On the soft, muddy, bomb-marked battlefields, horses were the logical means of carrying loads of ammunition up to gun emplacements. They often pulled the artillery itself into place. And when the artillery had done its worst, horses pulled ambulances, taking the casualties from the field of battle. Like the soldiers, these horses suffered terribly. The muddy conditions of fields blasted for months by shells made the prospect of a broken leg very real; at the same time, the shells themselves represented a hazard. One army veterinarian estimated that more than 120,000 horses were treated for wounds during a single year of the war. Between 1914 and 1916, the British army purchased more than one million animals for use in the war.

From time to time, mounted cavalry units still engaged in battle. The Russians entered World War I with 36 cavalry divisions; the British had 28. The French, German, and Turkish armies each had substantial numbers of regiments of dragoons and lancers. Cavalry played a particular role in the Palestine campaign of 1917–18 that pitted the British against the Turks; a force including 12,000 British sabers won a decisive victory. Yet in many instances the cavalry was found to be more hindrance than help. Russia's cavalry force was assigned so wide an area to patrol that it had to be transported by train to be of any value. It took four times as many trains to move a cavalry unit as an equal number of infantrymen.

During the Battle of Amiens in 1918, the Allies sent three divisions of cavalry onto the field along with three brigades of tanks, vehicles that became the horses' battlefield successors. The horse units scored some casualties against an enemy already weakened by the tanks. But overall the tactic failed because the horses and tanks got in each other's way.

At the battle of Huj, cavalry units charged two batteries of artillery across a half mile of open ground and succeeded in overcoming the enemy position. Australian cavalry used a mounted charge to counterattack German and Turkish units holding a bridgehead in 1918. They forced the Turks to retreat and then defeated the Germans. Although nobody knows for sure, it is possible that these represented the last instances of a cavalry charge in organized warfare.

Perhaps the cavalry horse's final moment of gallantry came during the early days of World War II. That war began when Hitler sent his mechanized Panzer units storming into Poland, where they were met by three regiments of Polish light horses, 27 regiments of lancers, and 10 additional cavalry regiments. The Poles had no chance, and within a matter of weeks the Panzers had destroyed almost all of that great cavalry on their drive into the Polish capital of Warsaw. But a small band of 300 cavalrymen continued the war on horseback as guerrilla fighters. Finally, even that band was wiped out and its leader shot by a German firing squad. The Polish cavalry had faced overwhelming odds, but at the same time, they exhibited that never-say-die spirit that has always marked the cavalry.

One American unit actually fought on horseback during World War II. That was a regiment of the 26th Cavalry, which was stationed in the Philippine islands when war broke out in 1941. The 842 officers and men of this unit largely served as mounted scouts following the Japanese invasion. They waged one memorable battle, defending the town of Binalonan against a tank assault at a cost of nearly half their manpower. By early 1942, conditions had become so bad and supplies so short for the island's defenders that the 26th was forced to turn over its horses to be used as food. The cavalrymen continued to fight until the island's surrender on April 9, 1942.

From that point on, cavalry combat in the Pacific was limited to a few small engagements. In one fierce 1942 battle, 60 sabers from an Indian regiment chased a larger Japanese force. Almost all the horsemen from India were killed.

By the end of World War II, the only effective cavalry force belonged to the Soviets, who conducted long-range raids behind German lines. These troops, which numbered nearly 20,000, not only harassed the invaders, but once the tide of battle turned, they also took part in the successful Soviet advance into Germany in 1945.

The last U.S. cavalry horse was a bay gelding named Chief, who was assigned to Fort Riley's cavalry school in 1941. He lived at the post until his death on May 24, 1968. Chief was buried near the Old Trooper monument at the post's Cavalry Parade Field. Hundreds of troops took part in the funeral, and hundreds more spectators lined the field to witness the passing not only of a horse but also of an entire way of military life.

c. 1500 B.C.   Ramses II creates the first organized military cavalry

c.700 B.C.   The saddle is developed by the Scythians

c. 400 B.C.   Philip of Macedonia develops the cavalry charge

1066 A.D.   William of Normandy crosses the English Channel with a large armored cavalry and defeats Harold to become the first King of England

1415   In the last great battle of knightly forces, 5,000 troops led by Henry V of England defeat a French force of 20,000 by employing lighter, swifter mounts

1778   Polish Count Casimir Pulaski is appointed the first commander of American cavalry during the Revolutionary War

1794   A force of U.S. dragoons defeats a union of Indian tribes at Fallen Timbers, Ohio; this is the first direct confrontation between the American cavalry and the Indians

1846   The Mexican War, the largest cavalry conflict on the American continent, breaks out between Mexico and the United States

1849   The discovery of gold in California spurs the westward expansion movement, causing the development of new frontier cavalry posts designed to provide protection to the settlers

1854   The Charge of the Light Brigade is repulsed by Russian artillery during the battle for Balaclava in the Crimean War

1866   The 7th Cavalry is given the mission of protecting frontier settlements from Indians

1892   The first Cavalry School is established at Fort Riley, Kansas

1898   The Rough Riders in a charge up San Juan Hillin Cuba

1939   The Polish cavalry is wiped out trying to halt the invading Nazi Panzers and infantry

1968   Chief, the last cavalry mount, dies at Fort Riley, Kansas

GLOSSARY

Cavalier—specifically, a defender of King Charles I during the "glorious revolution" of the 1600s in England; cavaliers were distinguished by their flamboyant dress and dashing manner

Cavalry—a group of mobile troops, usually mounted on horseback, although capable of fighting either mounted or on foot

Cavalry charge—the quick and mass movement of mounted soldiers toward a fixed enemy

Chariot—the earliest known cavalry conveyance, chariots were used by the Egyptian military during the time of the pharaohs to move spear-carrying soldiers on flat battle plains

Cuirassier—a cavalryman distinguished by the cuirass, a piece of defensive armor that covers the entire upper part of the trunk; cuirassiers were common cavalry units in the 16th through 19th centuries

Dragoon—a lightly armored, quick-striking, cavalryman of the 16th through 18th centuries; by the 19th century, especially in the United States, the term "dragoon" was virtually synonymous with cavalryman

Hussar—a brilliantly uniformed member of a lightly armored cavalry unit; originally from 16th century Hungary, whose gentry were required to support one cavalryman for every 20 acres of property they owned

Lancer—a cavalryman (or squad) armed principally or entirely with a lance, as opposed to a saber or handgun

McClellan Saddle—the type of saddle that was standard issue in the U.S. military between the late 1850s and the end of the horse cavalry in the 1940s; the McClellan saddle was named after its inventor, Civil War General George McClellan, who modeled it after saddles he saw being used during the Crimean War in Europe in the 1850s

Saber—a heavy, one-edged cavalry sword with a thick, often curved blade; although cavalrymen used many weapons through the ages, the saber is the one most closely identified with the cavalry

Yellowleg—a popular term for an American cavalryman

Ambrus, Victor. *Horses in Battle.* New York: Oxford University Press, 1975.

Ellis, John. Cavalry: *The History of Mounted Warfare.* New York: Putnam, 1978.

Herr, Major General John K., and Edward Wallace. *The Story of the U.S. Cavalry.* Boston: Little, Brown & Co., 1953.

Steffen, Randy. *The Horse Soldier.* (4 vols.) Norman, Oklahoma: University of Oklahoma Press, 1979.

Wormser, Richard. *The Yellowlegs: The Story of the U.S. Cavalry.* New York: Doubleday, 1966.

BILL FELBER is executive editor of *The Manhattan Mercury*, a daily newspaper in Manhattan, Kansas, and the author of several books, magazine and journal articles on topics as diverse as journalism education and major league baseball. This is his first publication on the subject of the cavalry.